11064646257

World Crafts and Recipes

Recipe and Craft Guide to

FRANCE

Amelia LaRoche

Mitchell Lane

P.O. Box 196
Hockessin, Delaware 19707
Visit us on the web: www.mitchelllane.com
Comments? email us: mitchelllane@mitchelllane.com

Mitchell Lane

World Crafts and Recipes

Recipe and Craft Guide to:
The Caribbean • China • **France**
India • Indonesia • Israel • Italy
Japan • South Africa

Copyright © 2011 by Mitchell Lane Publishers

All rights reserved. No part of this book
may be reproduced without written permission
from the publisher. Printed and bound in the
United States of America.

PUBLISHER'S NOTE: The facts on which the story
in this book is based have been thoroughly
researched. Documentation of such research
can be found on page 60. While every possible
effort has been made to ensure accuracy, the
publisher will not assume liability for damages
caused by inaccuracies in the data, and
makes no warranty on the accuracy of the
information contained herein.

To reflect current usage, we have chosen to
use the secular era designations BCE
("before the common era") and CE ("of the
common era") instead of the traditional
designations BC ("before Christ") and AD
(*anno Domini*, "in the year of the Lord").

**Library of Congress
Cataloging-in-Publication Data**

LaRoche, Amelia.
  Recipe and craft guide to France / by Amelia
LaRoche.
     p. cm. — (World crafts and recipes)
  Includes bibliographical references and index.
  ISBN 978-1-58415-936-0 (library bound)
  1. Cookery, French—Juvenile literature. 2.
Handicraft—France—Juvenile literature. I. Title.
  TX719.L33 2010
  641.5941--dc22
                                                 2010008949

Printing   2   3   4   5   6   7   8   9

                                              PLB / PLB2

CONTENTS

France is a magical country with a lot to offer visitors. It's the most popular tourist destination on earth! In fact, more people *visit* France than live there. The country has a population of about 60 million, and more than 79 million people traveled there in 2008. Tourists want to see the popular landmarks there, like the soaring Eiffel Tower and the Louvre Museum, where the famous *Mona Lisa* painting charms awestruck crowds with her mysterious smile.

Visitors sleep overnight in châteaus, castles, and cozy inns tucked into walled cities. They romp on the sunny beaches along the Mediterranean coast. They ski in the French Alps. They raft on France's rivers. They hike through its orchards, vineyards, and lush forests. France even has Disneyland Paris, where people line up for the rides and food.

People in France have a lot in common with those in the United States. Citizens of both countries elect their leaders; they enjoy a free press, which means they can print unpopular truths without fear of getting in trouble; and their children go to public schools where religion is not allowed to affect what is taught.

The two countries have helped each other during wartime. If it weren't for France, the United States might not have won its revolution against Great Britain. And if it weren't for the United States, France might still be occupied by Nazi Germany.

The country has twenty-two regions throughout its 210,000 square miles. It also has four overseas regions, holdovers from when France controlled a far-flung empire. Two are Guadeloupe and Martinique in the Caribbean Sea.

The French are famous for loving the arts. Some of the great painters of the ages lived there, including Degas, Matisse, and Seurat. Its great writers include Sartre, Beauvoir, and Prudhomme, who won the first Nobel Prize for literature.

Located in western Europe, France is called *L'Hexagone,* because its mainland has six sides like a hexagon. The second-largest country in Europe, it shares borders with Belgium, Luxembourg, Germany, Switzerland, Italy, and Spain. England lies just across a narrow channel of water. West of France is the Atlantic Ocean, and to the southeast is the Mediterranean Sea, where France's Corsica Island is nestled.

The people have an appetite for fine wine and delicious food, from crusty croissants to coq au vin, which is chicken stewed in wine. They share long weekend meals with friends and relatives, when conversation flows freely.

They're also famous for being very chic, which means fashionable. Some of the best clothing designers in the world have been French, from Coco Chanel to Christian Lacroix.

French inventors have contributed braille, the hot-air balloon, and the movie theater. Louis Pasteur discovered that germs cause disease, one of the most important medical breakthroughs ever made.

Taxes are high in France, but the people get a lot for their money. They enjoy free health care. Kids who make passing grades can go to college practically for free. Workers enjoy lots of vacation time. Many take off the month of August and flock to the countryside. More people in France own a second house than any other country's citizens.

The crafts in this book are organized loosely around some major eras in French history. The recipes are simple, so even beginning cooks can try their hand in the kitchen. Enjoy, and *vive la France!*

Create a Lascaux Painting

Early signs of human life in France date back about 700,000 years, when *Homo erectus* spread from Africa into Europe. Around 35,000 years ago, a new type of human showed up: Homo sapiens. Homo sapiens wore jewelry, made art, and hunted with great skill.

One of the most exciting examples of Paleolithic art is found in the Lascaux cave in southwest France. In 1940, four teenaged boys squirmed into a small opening to the cave and were stunned to find hundreds upon hundreds of images painted and carved on the walls deep inside.

The cave was closed to tourists in 1963 after so many crowded in that their breath damaged the paintings. A replica was built nearby in an old quarry. There, visitors can get a feeling for what those original painters felt thousands of years ago, when they put down their tools and stepped back to admire their work.

You'll Need:

large sheet of white drawing paper
coffee or tea grounds
water
charcoal drawing stick
red or orange poster paint
paintbrushes

The images throughout the multi-chambered Lascaux cave are about 16,000 years old and show humans, horses, stags, bears, and other animals. There are also abstract designs that some experts believe may be charts of the stars.

Make your "cave wall" by crinkling a large sheet of paper into a loose ball and then smoothing it flat. Put it in the sink and pour coffee or tea grounds over it. Add a little water and smear the grounds around, being careful not to rip the paper. Wipe off the excess grounds, and hang your paper to dry. After the paper dries, press it flat with the palms of your hands.

If you can, visit the Lascaux web site, and look at more cave paintings before you start your own.

Use a charcoal stick to draw the outline of an animal such as an aurochs, one of the huge wild cows that once lived in Europe and other parts of the world. Make the animal big for added drama. Dab on poster paint to partially fill in your drawing. You can also use the paint to make dots and lines, like the ones found in the original paintings.

Cool Secrets for Creating Great Crafts

- Read through the instructions—all the way—before you start. This tip can be hard to follow, because you might be so eager to start, you'll dive right in. That's the right spirit! But read all the way through anyway. You'll be glad you did.

- Gather all your materials first. A missing item might make you stop halfway through, and then you won't feel like finishing. Seeing a half-finished project lying around stinks.

- Protect your work surface. Lay down newspaper or a plastic tablecloth. (This is a step your parents will be glad you took!) Wear old clothes.

- Be creative. You might think of a great new step to add or a twist that gives the craft your personal touch. While you're at it, learn from your mistakes. Try a craft a few times to get it right. Your craft doesn't have to look like the one in the picture to be great.

- Be careful. When the instructions tell you to get help from an adult, you know what you should do? You guessed it. *Get help from an adult!*

- Clean up right away. It's much easier to clean paintbrushes, wipe down surfaces, and wash tools (including your hands) while the mess is fresh. Plus, when you ask for permission to start a new project, you can remind your parents that you cleaned up last time. (Add a "pretty please" if you think it will help). You could also ask your parents to join you. Crafts are even *more* fun when someone does them with you.

- As you go about your everyday activities, save things that might be good for your projects. Shoeboxes, toilet paper rolls, ribbon and tissue paper from a gift—these can all be used to make crafts that you'll enjoy keeping or giving to friends and family.

- The final secret? Have fun! If you don't enjoy it, there's no point in crafting.

Make a Claudian Tablet Gift Box

The Celts settled in France around 500 BCE, during the Bronze and Iron ages. They expanded through Gaul, which today is France, Belgium, and regions beyond. They had priests, called Druids, and they believed in reincarnation.

Around 125 BCE, Romans claimed the southern fringe of France. Julius Caesar brought the rest of Gaul under Roman control during the Gallic Wars (58 to 51 BCE). Gaul prospered under Rome for the next two centuries during the Pax Romana, or "Roman Peace." Lively cities full of public buildings, beautiful amphitheaters, and stone bathhouses sprang up.

In 48 CE, Emperor Claudius persuaded Rome to give the "long-haired" Gauls membership in his Senate. His speech was recorded on a massive sheet of bronze that stood about nine feet high and weighed more than a thousand pounds. The Claudian Tablet is now displayed in Lyons, where Claudius was born.

You can use the look of the Claudian Tablet to decorate a box that will be ideal for holding a gift or other items.

You'll Need:

cardboard box
alphabet stickers
black and orange craft paint
paintbrush

Find a small cardboard box, or buy one at any craft store.

Mix the black and orange paint together. You don't have to blend them perfectly. Slight changes in the tone will mimic the look of aged bronze. Paint the box, and let it dry.

Peel off capital-letter stickers and press them onto the box to mimic the lettering on the tablet. You can copy the order of the letters shown here, or make up your own order. The goal is not to write Latin; it's simply to re-create the look of the tablet.

The Claudian Tablet

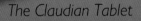

Rome's mighty empire began to crumble, and by the fourth century CE, fierce Barbarian invaders were sweeping into Gaul from the east.

From the fifth century on, during the Dark Ages, Barbarian tribes began settling throughout the area. The name France comes from a Germanic tribe known as the Franks.

The Frankish Merovingian (mayr-oh-VIN-jee-un) dynasty ruled from the fifth to the eighth century. Clovis was the first Frankish king to unite all the tribes in Gaul. He converted to the Roman Catholic faith.

The High Middle Ages were ushered in by the first true French dynasty, the Carolingians (kayr-oh-LIN-jee-uns), who ruled from the eighth to the tenth century. Charlemagne is one of the best-known Carolingians. He couldn't read or write, but he still managed to run the country with an iron fist.

During the rule of both dynasties, the Catholic Church wielded great power in France. Monks living in monasteries tamed the land, creating new ways of farming and growing grapes for wine. Nuns vowed chastity and poverty. From serf to lord, and from birth to death, most French people had lives that revolved around the church.

One of the most magical places in southwest France is Le Puy. It lies in a basin of mountains, and throughout the area, plugs of lava-rock rise from the land like natural pyramids. Some are topped by dramatic statuary, and one features a medieval chapel.

Le Puy began to attract people on religious pilgrimages, including Charlemagne, who was the first of thirteen kings to visit. Thousands of pilgrims still go there, and so do tourists. They enjoy strolling through the hilly town, with its picturesque cobbled lanes and rich mansions. Some of its buildings have doorways with elaborate carved masks.

You can make a carved mask like the ones found in Le Puy. The ingredients here are enough for two masks. This project is more fun with two people, and it's helpful to have one person pour the wet plaster of Paris while the other person holds a spoon to keep the plaster from gushing down so hard it moves the sand around.

A Carolingian

You'll Need:

2 boxes to hold sand (the size of the containers depends on the size of the mask you want to make; the smaller mask pictured was made in a wooden box that held Clementine oranges, and the larger mask was made in a cardboard box about one foot wide, two feet long, and seven inches deep)

plastic wrap or newspaper to line the boxes, if necessary

5-gallon bucket of builder's sand

trowel

4-pound container of plaster of Paris

plastic bucket

water

scooping and poking tools, including a large spoon

2 paper clips

old paintbrush or toothbrush

Line the boxes with plastic wrap or newspaper to keep the sand from leaking out. Use the trowel to fill the boxes with builder's sand. Smooth the sand at the top.

To create the mask molds, scoop out sand in the center, until the hole is the general size of the mask you want. Use your tools to make details, like bulging eyes, fat cheeks, horns, teeth, and decorative whirls and blobs.

In the plastic bucket, mix the plaster of Paris with water according to the directions on the package. Read the directions carefully! If you add too much water, you can't go back and fix your mistake.

Pour the plaster into the molds. One person should hold a large spoon under the flow of the plaster so that it doesn't gush down and move the sand around.

After the plaster has set for a minute, bend a paperclip into a T by pulling the shorter loop to a 90-degree angle. On the first mask, push the top of the T into the plaster, leaving the shorter, looped end—the stick of the T—poking out. Repeat on the other mask. The masks will hang from these paperclips.

Let the plaster dry for several hours, regardless of the drying time listed on the container. It's best to leave it overnight.

Remove the plaster masks from the sand, then use an old paintbrush or toothbrush to whisk off the excess sand. Ask an adult to hammer two sturdy nails into the wall so that you can hang your masks and enjoy seeing them gaze back at you.

Pouring the plaster onto a spoon will keep it from ruining your mold. The finished mask will be the opposite of the shapes you press into the sand. To make bulging eyes, for instance, you need to gouge holes in the sand.

Make a Stained-Glass Window

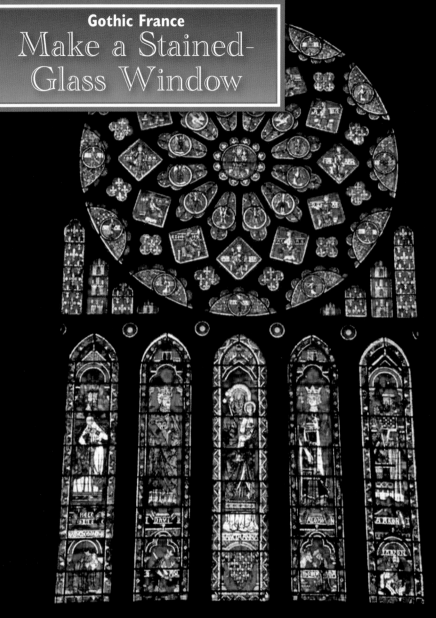

The High Middle Ages in France gave birth to Gothic architecture, which became known as "the French style." Rich merchants seeking favor from the church paid for skilled masons to build towering Gothic cathedrals. People from all over Europe flocked to see their soaring ceilings and beautiful stained-glass windows.

Round stained-glass windows are called rose windows. You can make a rose window that will add beauty to your own home, even if it isn't quite as dramatic as a Gothic cathedral.

You'll Need:

1 large sheet of black poster board or construction paper
round template, like a dinner plate, pot lid, or plastic lid—
depending on how big you want to make your window
pencil
scissors
glue stick
tissue paper of various colors
clear tape

Place your template on a sheet of black poster board or construction paper. Trace around it with a pencil. Cut out the paper circle.

Fold the circle in half or in quarters. Cut out unusual and interesting shapes. Make sure you don't cut into the outer edges of the circle! The thicker your edges are, the easier it is to add tissue paper later. Open the circle and examine your design. Refold it in a different way and cut a few more shapes (make sure you don't cut into the shapes that are already there).

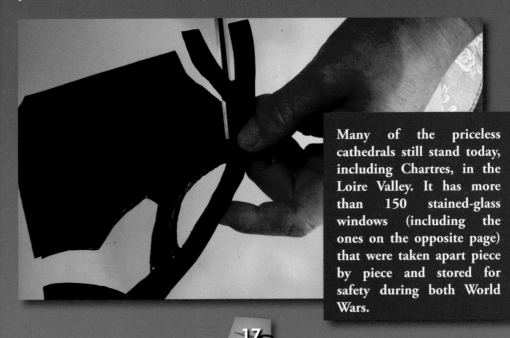

Many of the priceless cathedrals still stand today, including Chartres, in the Loire Valley. It has more than 150 stained-glass windows (including the ones on the opposite page) that were taken apart piece by piece and stored for safety during both World Wars.

Open your circle. Cut out a piece of tissue paper that is slightly larger than one of the holes in the circle. Rub the glue stick around the hole in the circle, and place the tissue paper on top of it.

Repeat for each hole, varying the color of the tissue paper. Make sure that when you add more tissue paper, you add it to the same side of the circle.

Use clear tape to hang your circle in a sunny window, with the side you glued facing out.

You can make smaller "windows" to use as Christmas ornaments, too.

Make a Pomander

The Middle Ages ended with the Hundred Years' War, which saw France and England fighting for control of French land. The war raged on and off from 1337 to 1453. It had a terrible effect on the French people. Even when truces were made, soldiers from both sides plundered the French countryside, taking whatever they wanted from peasants who were already on the brink of starvation because of crop failures.

After a bloody battle in Agincourt in 1415, England controlled most of northern France. It seemed as if English soldiers and their deadly longbows would eventually conquer all of France.

In 1429, an illiterate thirteen-year-old peasant girl claimed she heard the voices of saints telling her to rescue the French people. Wearing a suit of white armor, Joan of Arc rallied the war-weary French troops and led them to victories in Orléans and Patay, turning the tide in France's favor. She was eventually imprisoned by the English and executed as a heretic, but her efforts to save France made her a national hero.

One of the things that devastated France as much as the war was the Black Death, a pandemic that peaked in Europe between 1348 and 1350 and wiped out at least a third of the population. It was most likely a result of bubonic plague, spread by rats carrying infected fleas. Over a three-month period in 1349, the Black Death killed 800 people every day in Paris. In the countryside, entire villages were wiped out.

The word *pomander* comes from the French *pomme d'ambre,* which some people translate as "amber apple" or "golden apple." Pomanders became especially popular when the Black Death ran rampant. Because sanitation was so bad in the Middle Ages, a stench lingered over the towns and cities. Some people believed that the Black Death was caused by the repulsive odors. They hoped a sweet-smelling pomander would drive away disease.

You can make a sweet-smelling pomander, too. It might not ward off the plague, but it will make your closet smell nice.

You'll Need:

1 piece of fruit—apples, lemons, and oranges all work well
1 large bottle of whole cloves
1 teaspoon cinnamon
1 teaspoon nutmeg
a few drops of sandalwood oil (available at health food stores)
brown paper bag
masking tape
1 foot of ribbon
knitting needle or small scissors with a sharp point

Use masking tape to mark one-quarter sections on a piece of fruit. With a knitting needle or scissors, poke holes into the parts of the fruit that aren't covered by tape. Push cloves into the holes. The closer together the cloves, the prettier your pomander will look.

Put the cinnamon, nutmeg, and sandalwood oil into a brown paper bag. Drop in your fruit and swish it around until it's coated. Leave the fruit in the bag for a couple of weeks, shaking it daily to recoat it in the spices. Keep the bag in a cool, dry place.

Once your pomander is dried out, remove the tape. Crisscross a piece of ribbon over the open spaces and tie it in a knot at the top. Then use the ribbon to tie the pomander to the rod in your closet.

Simple pomanders were hollowed out of wood, but rich people wore pomanders made of gold and studded with jewels. They were often divided into sections, like an orange, and each section was filled with herbs and wax-based perfumes.

The French invaded Italy in 1494. When they returned, they brought home the ideals of the Italian Renaissance. Over the next two hundred years, the monarchy became more powerful than ever, but individuals began to earn greater respect as well.

One of the great accomplishments of the French Renaissance was the construction of more than 300 *châteaux* (shah-TOH) in the Loire Valley. French royalty and rich citizens spent much of their time in these huge and elaborate buildings, which were built for pleasure, not defense.

You can make a model château out of one manila file folder and four toilet paper rolls.

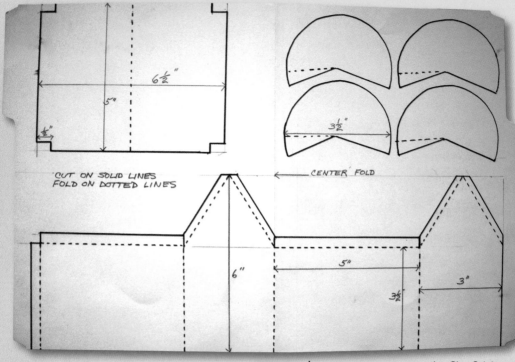

A pattern on a manila file folder

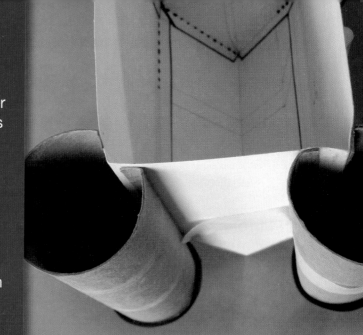

This is how the turrets should be attached.

Draw the pattern on a manila file folder, using the measurements shown. The roof is on the upper left. The turret roofs are on the upper right. The body of the château is at the bottom.

Cut out the pieces along the solid black lines. (Don't cut where you see pencil lines on the pattern—they are there to show the measurements.)

After the pieces are cut out, fold them on the dotted lines. To get a really crisp fold, place a ruler against the dotted line and fold the paper over it, pressing down hard.

On the body of the château, use a very thin line of white glue on the tab you created by folding along the dotted line on the left side. Press the tab onto the inside of the right side. Use a small piece of masking tape to hold the body together while the glue dries.

Put the roof on the château and see where the edges meet. Remove the roof and run a bead of glue around it where it will meet the body. Put it on, and let the glue dry.

Cut a toilet paper roll lengthwise. Make inward-facing folds on both sides. Put a thin bead of glue on the outside of each tab and glue the roll to the body, making sure it's flush at the bottom. Use a piece of masking tape to hold it in place while the glue dries. Repeat with the other three rolls.

Fold a cone-shaped turret roof. Glue the folded tab in place. Use a small piece of masking tape to hold it together while the glue dries. Repeat with the other three turret roofs.

Place one turret on a toilet paper roll to see where it touches. Remove it and run a bead of glue around it where it will meet the turret. Put it on and let the glue dry. Repeat with the other three roofs.

Once the glue is dry on every part of your château, carefully peel off the masking tape. Paint it any color you like. Many châteaus in France are made of yellowish or brown stone. Others are gray. Many have black roofs.

After the paint has dried, cut windows out of black construction paper and glue them onto the turrets and walls of your château.

For added fun, you can glue a piece of green construction paper to a piece of cardboard as a base for your château. Roll up a couple of small pieces of modeling clay and poke in tiny branches, and it will look as if there are trees in front. Once the clay has hardened, paint it green.

Have fun painting your château. You can use different colors to mimic the look of stones or bricks. Add "trees" to the property. This one was snipped from a garden plant.

Frame Your Family, Versailles Style

In the seventeenth century, a cruel and cunning prime minister named Cardinal Richelieu paved the way for the absolute rule of Louis XIV. Known as the Sun King, Louis began construction on an elaborate palace at Versailles. The expensive palace, and his endless wars, left the country in financial danger. So while this century was known as the *Grand Siècle*—or Grand Century—it wasn't exactly grand for everyone.

The 700-room Versailles palace has thousands of beautiful paintings hanging in gilded frames. You can make your own "gold" frame for a copy of your favorite photo. If you use a photograph of your family, you can paste crowns onto the photo to create your own royal family. But let's hope there won't be a revolution in your house!

You'll Need:

Sculpey baking clay
cardboard
ruler
pencil or marker
scissors
a photograph to frame (a picture of your family or a pet is a great choice—get permission to use the photo, because once it's in the frame, it can't be removed)
table knife, fork, and other tools you can use to make patterns in the clay
cookie sheet
oven mitts
white glue
clear tape
gold craft paint
paintbrush
construction paper and markers (you'll only need these if you decide to "crown" the subjects in your photograph)
hammer and nail (optional)

A golden frame fit for just about any family member's portrait.

Measure your photograph. Then cut the cardboard so that it's one inch wider and longer than the photo. If your photo is five by seven inches, the cardboard should be six by eight inches. Save the leftover cardboard.

Place the photo in the center of the cardboard and trace around it. Remove the photo.

Roll out four lengths of Sculpey and press them onto the frame drawn on the cardboard in an even, quarter-inch-thick layer. Make the Sculpey overlap the line you drew so that your photo's edges won't show once the photo is in the frame.

Use a table knife, fork, or other tool to make patterns in the frame. Use more clay to decorate the frame. Roll up small balls and press the flat side of a table knife into them to make interesting blobs. Roll a long, thin strand of clay and curve it along the frame, then put leaf-shaped pieces on top to make a vine. Add a large circle at the top of the frame and roll thin pieces of dough to form the first letter of your name. The fancier your decorations are, the more interesting your frame will be.

Gently slide the clay frame off the cardboard and onto a cookie sheet. **With an adult's help,** use an oven to bake the frame according to the directions on the package of Sculpey. When it's finished baking, ask the adult to use oven mitts and remove the tray from the oven. Let the frame cool and harden overnight.

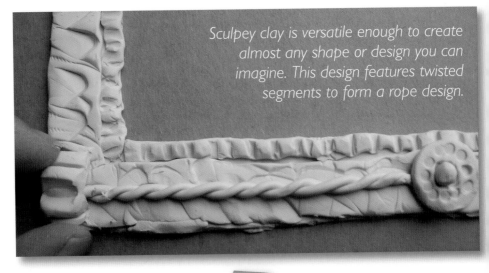

Sculpey clay is versatile enough to create almost any shape or design you can imagine. This design features twisted segments to form a rope design.

Inset: The cardboard placement for the back of your frame. Pictured: When you've sculpted your frame just right, it's time to paint!

Paint the hardened frame with gold craft paint. You may need to apply two coats. Be sure to get paint into all the nooks and crannies.

Use a small piece of clear tape to fix the photograph to the cardboard. Put a thin line of white glue around the back of the entire frame. Press the cardboard onto it.

Use the leftover cardboard to make a stand for your frame. Cut a strip about two inches wide and five inches long. Trim the edges so that they form opposite angles. Bend a half-inch cardboard tab at one end, and glue the tab to the back of the frame. Trim the other end until the frame is standing at an angle you like.

You can also cut a one-inch tab of cardboard and punch a hole in one end. Bend the cardboard in half and glue the half without the hole to the frame. The half with the hole should be on top. You can use this to hang your frame from a small nail in the wall. Ask an adult to bang in the nail with a hammer.

To really make your family look like royalty, you can decorate your photograph by cutting crowns from construction paper. Use a marker to draw a few jewels onto the crowns, then glue them onto everyone's heads!

Sculpt a Christmas Santon

Most of the people in France were commoners, and by the eighteenth century, they were beginning to resent the privileged lifestyles of the nobles and clergymen. Enlightenment philosophers like Voltaire and Rousseau fanned the flames by challenging the aristocratic order. Essays by these free thinkers called for equal rights, and they were read throughout Europe and as far away as the American colonies.

New ideas and increasing financial turmoil combined like thunderclouds, and in 1789, lightning struck in the form of revolution. On July 14, a mob stormed Paris's Bastille prison, which was seen as a place of political oppression. The revolutionaries issued a Declaration of the Rights of Man, calling for an end to the class system. It embodied the principles of *"Liberté, Egalité, Fraternité"*—Liberty, Equality, Fraternity—which later became the French motto.

During the Revolution, churches were forced to close, and their large nativity scenes were forbidden. People began to make tiny, hand-painted crèche figures out of clay to display in their homes.

An artist in Marseille named Jean-Louis Lagnel invented molds for *santons*. He included the typical figures such as Jesus, Joseph, and Mary, and he added characters from village life such as the fishwife, the blind man, and the chestnut seller. The molds made it possible to churn out many figures, and more people were able to have home crèches.

You can put a twist on the *santon* by making a Père Noel, or Father Christmas. If you push an ornament hanger into his head while the clay is still moist, you can hang him from a Christmas tree.

A Santa santon

You'll Need:

air-dry clay
table knife
red, black, white, and gold poster paint
paintbrush
jar of water
hot glue gun
ornament hanger (optional)

Roll a thick length of air-dry clay for Santa's body. Use a table knife to make a line that gives him the appearance of having legs. Press on his boots. Make sure the body will stand on its own.

Roll a ball for the head. Use small pieces of clay to make a belt and belt buckle, Santa hat, and the details for Santa's face: nose, mustache, and beard.

Roll smaller lengths for Santa's arms. Press them at the bottom and use the knife to cut the pressed part, so that Santa's mittens will have thumbs. Press the arms onto his body. Use a blob of clay to make Santa's toy sack.

Press an ornament hanger into Santa's head if you plan to hang him from your Christmas tree.

Let the clay dry overnight. Use poster paints on your Santa. You can mix red and white paint for his face. Paint his belt buckle gold.

A shop selling santons

Make Napoleon's Hat

The Revolution ended when Napoleon Bonaparte marched into Paris and was crowned First Consul. In 1804 he took the title of Emperor Napoleon I. He expanded his empire throughout most of western Europe, and he put his brothers and sisters on the thrones of the countries he conquered.

Napoleon was defeated in Russia in 1812 and then at Waterloo in 1815. He was replaced by Louis XVIII, who was overthrown by Charles X. The way Charles ruled reminded people of the old, oppressive regime, and the people started the July Revolution of 1830. A new king, Louis Philippe, was elected. His reign lasted eighteen years and was a period of growth and prosperity.

The Napoleonic clan made a short comeback after 1848. Napoleon's nephew, Louis Napoleon, became president of the Second Republic. In 1852, he became emperor as Napoleon III. During his reign, Paris was modernized, and the industrial revolution of France began.

You can fold the first Napoleon's famous hat. You'll need a large sheet of black poster board. Follow the folding instructions shown here.

Embroider a Lavender Sachet or Pouch

The decades leading up to World War I were a *belle epoque,* or golden age, for the French. Electricity and vaccination against disease made life easier for everyone. More than 3 million people flooded into Paris for the 1889 Universal Exhibition to see the beautiful—and controversial—Eiffel Tower.

During World War II, the Third Republic collapsed. Part of France, including Paris, was occupied by German soldiers until the country's Liberation in 1944. The Free French Forces were led by Charles de Gaulle, who later became the country's eighteenth president.

In the decades after the 1950s, French society changed as the number of peasant farmers fell and more and more people worked as teachers, doctors, lawyers, civil servants, and pioneers of the World Wide Web. Today France is one of 27 countries in the European Union, whose aim is "Peace, prosperity and freedom for its 498 million citizens—in a fairer, safer world."

Despite its modernization, France still has agriculture at its heart. In July, the lavender fields of Provence in southern France burst into fragrant, purple life. This sweet-smelling herb has been in use for thousands of years and is prized for its use in perfume and medicine. King Charles VI is said to have demanded lavender-filled pillows wherever he went.

Combine the best of old and new France in a sachet that you can tuck into a clothes drawer or a pouch that can nestle next to your pillow after you make your bed in the morning. These projects include simple embroidery, a craft at which the French excel, and materials you can buy at any modern store with a crafting section. One of the stitches is a French knot.

Sachet

2 pieces of felt that are 6 inches square (you can use any color felt you like; it's nice to have different colors for the top and bottom)

scissors

embroidery needle

green, purple, red, and pink embroidery floss

green and purple markers

paper

small amount of polyester stuffing

handful of dried lavender (from a health food store or ordered online)

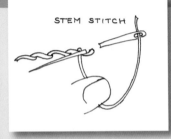

STEM STITCH

On a piece of paper, use a fine-point marker to draw a picture of lavender. With the needle, punch holes ¼ inch apart throughout the design. Place the paper on the piece of felt and dab the marker through the paper onto the felt. Use green marker for the stems and purple marker for the lavender flowers at the top.

Embroider the felt, using green floss and the stem stitch shown for the stems. Use purple floss to make French knots, as shown, for the lavender flowers. Use pink floss and the stem stitch to make a band that looks as if it is holding the stems together.

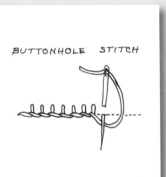

BUTTONHOLE STITCH

Put the two pieces of felt together and use the buttonhole stitch shown to join them. Leave a two-inch opening at the top. Stuff a small amount of polyester filling into each corner. Fill the center with dried lavender. Use the buttonhole stitch to close the sachet.

Pouch

2 ready-cut felt swatches in red and yellow (these come in squares of 11¾ by 9 inches at stores with a crafting section)
felt scraps in various colors
scissors (pinking sheers optional)
embroidery needle
green and red embroidery floss (other colors are optional)
green marker
paper
small amount of polyester stuffing
handful of dried lavender (from a health food store or ordered online)
1 piece of thin red ribbon about six inches long
beads or buttons (optional)

On a piece of paper, draw a design of stems and leaves. It's nice to make at least three sets. With the needle, punch holes

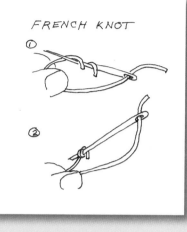

FRENCH KNOT

¼ inch apart throughout the design. Place the paper on the piece of yellow felt, with the longer side facing the top and bottom. Dab the green marker through the holes onto the felt.

Use green floss and the stem stitch shown to embroider the stems and leaves.

Cut small pieces of contrasting felt scraps into flower heads and attach them with French knots. You can use the floss colors you already have, or use other colors, like blue or white. You can also sew on a pretty bead or button to hold down a flower head.

Cut a scalloped shape at the top of the felt, or use pinking shears if you have them in the house. Fold the embroidered piece in half, and join the nine-inch sides together with the buttonhole stitch shown.

Cut out a circle from the red felt that is 4½ inches in diameter. Use the buttonhole stitch to attach it to the bottom of the yellow felt.

Fill the pouch with polyester stuffing and a handful of dried lavender. Tie it at the top with the red ribbon.

You can also use these instructions to make a pouch that can hold small treasures, such as seashells, marbles, or doll clothes.

FRENCH RECIPES

Do You Have the Chops to Be a Master Chef?

Some of the best chefs in the world train at the famous Cordon Bleu cooking school in Paris. The first class was held in 1896, and the organizers were very proud to offer a kitchen featuring the latest technology: electricity!

France is rightly known as a gastronomist's paradise. Western France is known for its bountiful seafood and salt-marsh lamb. Northeast France offers tangy sauerkraut with pork and home-brewed beer made from locally grown hops. Central France produces a bounty of cheeses, from rich blue cheese to mild Gruyéres that are melted into fondue sauce. In southwest France, cooks vie to produce the best cassoulet, a thick stew of white beans and sausage. In the south, hearty fish stews are served hot, and zesty tarts are made with locally grown lemons. Even farther south, the island of Corsica offers olive tapenade scooped onto fresh-baked bread.

Here are a few tips to make your time in the kitchen fun and delicious.

- Read through the recipe—*all the way*—before you start. Stopping halfway through the cooking process because you don't have the right ingredients or cookware is a waste of food. Plus, you'll still be hungry!
- Wear an apron. Wash your hands before you start.
- Be very careful! Always get help from an adult when you are using the oven, the stovetop, or sharp knives. Use oven mitts to lift hot baking sheets and pans. Protect the counter with a trivet before you set down a hot container.
- Clean up right away. The sooner you do it, the easier it will be.
- Once you've made a recipe successfully, you can experiment the next time. Change the ingredients. Use blueberries instead of raspberries, or honey instead of sugar.
- Finally, share your food with your friends and family. Seeing people enjoy your cooking is as much fun as enjoying it yourself!

Pain Perdu

Pain perdu means "lost bread," and it's called that because making it is a good way to use day-old bread that might normally be "lost" to the garbage pail. It's also called French toast. This recipe makes four pieces.

- 4 slices stale French bread
- 2 eggs
- 2 tablespoons milk
- ¼ teaspoon vanilla extract
- ¼ teaspoon cinnamon
- 1 tablespoon butter
  - maple syrup or honey as topping

In a shallow bowl, beat together the eggs and the milk. Stir in the vanilla and cinnamon. **Ask an adult** to help you bring a skillet to medium high heat, and add a pat of butter. The butter should sizzle.

Dip a piece of bread in the egg and milk mixture, coating it on both sides. Ask an adult to help you fry it in the skillet until it is golden. Then flip it over and cook the other side.

Repeat with the other three pieces of bread, adding a pat of butter to the skillet each time. If you want, you can ask an adult to preheat the oven to 250 degrees, so you can keep the French toast warm until all of the pieces are cooked.

Serve your French toast with maple syrup or honey.

Pain perdu

Crepes

Crepes are delicious for breakfast, lunch, or dessert! You can roll all sorts of things into them, like yogurt with fruit or lunchmeat with a thin slice of onion. You can spoon ice cream on top of a crepe, then dribble on chocolate sauce and a shake of powdered sugar.

Dessert crepes taste even better if you add a teaspoon of sugar and ¼ teaspoon of vanilla while you're mixing the ingredients. For a crepe you're going to serve with lunchmeats or vegetables, skip the sugar and vanilla, but add ⅛ teaspoon of pepper.

The ingredients here make about eight crepes. You don't have to make them all at once. You can keep the batter in the refrigerator for a day or two.

1 cup all-purpose flour
2 eggs
½ cup milk
½ cup water
¼ teaspoon salt
3 tablespoons butter

Melt two tablespoons of the butter in the microwave. Don't let it burn!

In a large mixing bowl, beat the eggs. Gradually stir in the milk and water. Add the butter and the salt. Beat all the ingredients until you have a smooth batter. Then mix in the flour, a little at a time. Stir the batter thoroughly, making sure there aren't any lumps.

Ask an adult to help you put a frying pan over medium high heat. Put a dab of the remaining butter in the frying pan and let it melt. When you add a dot of batter and it bubbles right away, the pan is hot enough.

Pour ¼ cup of batter into the frying pan. Swirl the pan around so that the batter coats it evenly. Cook the crepe for about two minutes, until the bottom is light brown. Flip it over with a spatula, and cook the other side until it's light brown.

With an adult's help, repeat these steps, including adding a dab of butter for each crepe, until you've made as many as you want. Serve your crepes while they're piping hot.

Celery Stuffed with Roquefort Cheese

This is a crunchy treat that might surprise you. Roquefort cheese is strong, but if you like it, you will want to try lots of different cheeses. This recipe makes about thirty pieces.

- 8   celery stalks
- ½   cup crumbled Roquefort cheese
- 3   tablespoons butter
- 1   tablespoon water
- ⅛   teaspoon salt
- ⅛   teaspoon pepper
- 1   tablespoon paprika

Cut the butter into tiny chunks. In a bowl, use a fork to mix the butter and cheese into a paste. Stir in the water, salt, and pepper. Place the bowl in the refrigerator.

Wash the celery in cold water, and cut off the tops and bottoms. Use a vegetable peeler to remove the strings from the back of each piece. Get the paste from the fridge and scoop it into the celery. Use a table knife to smooth it flat.

Sprinkle paprika very lightly over the top. Use a kitchen knife to cut the celery into 1½-inch lengths. Arrange the pieces on a large plate. You can place a few celery tops in a tiny vase and set it on the platter as decoration.

47

Sausage en Croute

Sausage en croute makes a great hors d'oeuvre, which is French for "appetizer" and means "apart from the main course." This recipe makes about sixteen pieces.

- 1 sheet of frozen puff pastry
- 2 six-inch sausages (vegetarians can use meat-substitute sausages)
- 1 egg
- 1 tablespoon water
  flour for the counter surface
  Dijon mustard as a topping

Thaw the frozen puff pastry for forty minutes. After the pastry has thawed, preheat the oven to 375°F.

Unfold the pastry and roll it out on a lightly floured surface until it's about one foot square. Cut the pastry in half crosswise.

Wrap each sausage in a piece of pastry. Fold the ends of the pastry over the sausage and pinch them shut.

Break the egg into a small bowl and beat it with the water. Brush it all over each pastry. Place the pastries on a cookie sheet and **ask an adult** to help you put them in the oven. Bake them for 40 minutes, until they are puffy and golden. **Ask an adult** to help you remove them from the oven.

Cut each sausage into bite-sized slices. Serve them warm with a dish of Dijon mustard.

Sausage en croute

Croque-Monsieur

Croque-monsieur translates as "Mister Crunchy." It's a delicious hot ham-and-cheese sandwich. You can make four with this recipe.

1	tablespoon butter
1½	tablespoons all-purpose flour
1	cup hot milk
½	teaspoon salt
¼	teaspoon black pepper
3	cups grated Gruyère cheese
¼	cup grated Parmesan cheese
8	slices of bread (peasant bread is especially good)
8	slices of ham
	Dijon mustard

Preheat the oven to 400°F.

Ask an adult to help you melt the butter over low heat in a small saucepan. Add the flour and stir it for a minute. Pour in the hot milk and whisk it constantly until the sauce is thick. Take the pan off the stove and add about half the Gruyère cheese and all of the Parmesan cheese. Set it aside.

Toast the bread on a baking sheet in the oven for a few minutes. Flip it over and toast it for another minute or so. **Ask an adult** for help with these steps.

Brush the toast with a light layer of mustard. Put two slices of ham on each of four pieces of bread. Sprinkle them with the rest of the Gruyère cheese. Put a little mustard on the other four pieces of bread. Place them on top of the first four pieces and the ham.

Scoop the warm cheese sauce over the four sandwiches. **Ask an adult** to put the sandwiches into the oven and bake them for another five minutes. Turn on the broiler and cook the sandwiches until the cheese sauce is bubbly and light brown at the edges. **Ask an adult** to take the baking sheet out of the oven.

Serve the sandwiches while they're hot!

Croque-Monsieur

Quiche

Quiche Lorraine is named after the Lorraine region and usually includes bacon, but you can add cheese instead.

1 frozen eight-inch piecrust
3 eggs
1 cup milk
1 cup grated cheddar cheese

Preheat the oven to 375°F.

Ask an adult to help you bake the piecrust for ten minutes and then remove it from the oven.

Beat together the eggs and the milk.

Sprinkle the grated cheese onto the piecrust. Pour in the egg and milk mixture. **Ask an adult** to help you bake the quiche for 45 minutes. Let it cool for a couple of minutes before you serve it.

Quiche

Pot au Feu

Pot au Feu means "pot on the fire." Many people make it with chicken, but this recipe calls for beef. Stew is great on a cold day. This one will serve four people (or three very hungry people).

1½ pounds stew beef (vegetarians can use beef strip substitutes)
2   tablespoons flour
1   tablespoon vegetable oil
1   can beef or vegetable stock
2   carrots
2   celery stalks
1   medium onion
2   large russet potatoes
1   clove garlic
1   teaspoon salt
1   teaspoon pepper

Cut the beef into chunks the size of a quarter. Coat the chunks in the flour. **Ask an adult** to help you heat the vegetable oil in a frying pan. Brown the beef in the oil.

Slice the carrots and celery, and chop the onion and potato into chunks. Mash and dice the garlic.

Put the beef stock, chopped vegetables, garlic, and browned beef in a large pot. Add the salt and pepper. **Ask an adult** to help you bring the pot to a boil. Then lower the heat all the way and let the stew simmer until the meat is cooked all the way through and the potatoes are soft.

Pommes Frites

Pommes frites is French for "fried potatoes," which we call French fries. You can make French fries at home, and they'll taste better than the ones from a fast-food restaurant. You will need lots of help from an adult, because you must use hot oil to make them.

6   russet potatoes
1   quart vegetable or peanut oil
    salt to taste
    ketchup or Dijon mustard as dipping sauce

Ask an adult to preheat a deep pot of oil to 325°F. Peel the potatoes, and cut them into finger-sized pieces.

Ask an adult to carefully drop the potatoes into the hot oil. Cook them for about five minutes, until they are golden. They should float to the top of the oil, but they should not stop sizzling. (If they do, they will be oily.) You may have to fry the potatoes in batches.

Ask an adult to remove the potatoes using a slotted spoon. Lay them on a plate lined with paper towels. Let them cool to room temperature.

Raise the temperature of the oil to 375°F.

Ask an adult to fry the potatoes again, for about two minutes, until they are crispy. **Have the adult** remove them from the oil and put them in a bowl lined with paper towels. Sprinkle on a little salt while the potatoes are hot. You can serve them with ketchup, but they're also good with Dijon mustard.

French Apple Pie

French apple pie is easier to make than you might think, especially if you use a prepared piecrust.

1   frozen eight-inch piecrust

Filling:
5   medium apples
½   cup sugar
3   tablespoons flour
¼   teaspoon ground nutmeg
¼   teaspoon ground cinnamon
    dash of salt

Topping:
1   cup flour
½   cup butter
½   cup brown sugar

Preheat the oven to 425°F. Cut the apples into dime-sized chunks. Put them into a large bowl and mix in the other filling ingredients. Pour the filling into the piecrust.

In another bowl, mix the topping ingredients until they are crumbly. Cover the pie with the topping. Bake the pie for 40 minutes. **Ask an adult** to remove the hot pie, and place aluminum foil over the top. Bake it for another 10 minutes.

Let it cool before slicing, because the apples will be very hot!

Three Kings Cake

A Christmastime treat is Three Kings Cake. It celebrates the visit by the three magi, or kings, to the Baby Jesus, and it is traditionally served on Epiphany, or January 6. The French like to hide something inside the cake, like an almond or a dried fava bean. Whoever gets that slice becomes royalty for a day, and everyone else in the house has to do his or her bidding!

- 2   sheets frozen puff pastry
- 10 ounces almond paste
- 1   almond or dried fava bean
      flour for the countertop
- 1   egg
- 1   teaspoon water

Preheat the oven to 350°F.

Roll out the sheets of puff pastry. Using a table knife, trace the bottom of the pie pan onto each pastry. Cut the circles out, and save the trimmings.

Place one sheet of pastry into the pie pan. Spread the almond paste on top. Put the almond or bean into the paste. Place the second sheet of pastry on top of the paste. Use the trimmings to decorate the top crust.

Beat the egg with the water. Brush it onto the top crust.

Ask an adult to put the pie into the oven and bake it for about 20 minutes, or until it is nicely browned on top.

Three Kings Cake

Further Reading

Books

Baude, Dawn-Michelle, Ph.D. *The Everything Kids' Learning French Book.* Avon, MA: Adams Media. 2008.

D'Harcourt, Claire. *Louvre Up Close.* San Francisco: Chronicle Books, 2007.

Neal, Lisa. *France: An Illustrated History.* New York: Hippocrene Books, 2001.

Uhlmann, Karen. *Paris for Kids.* Chicago: Xlibris Publishing, 2005.

Waldee, Lynne Marie. *Cooking the French Way: Revised and Expanded to Include New Low-Fat and Vegetarian Recipes.* Minneapolis: Lerner Publications, 2001.

Works Consulted

Allrecipes.com
  http://allrecipes.com/recipe/basic-crepes/detail.aspx?washelp=1&rid=954908#954908

Bailey, Rosemary, project editor. *France, DK Eyewitness Travel Guides.* New York: DK Publishing, Inc., 1994, with revisions in 2003.

Barefoot Contessa. "Croque Monsieur." *Food Network.com*
  http://www.foodnetwork.com/recipes/ina-garten/croque-monsieur-recipe/index.html

Bertholle, Louisette. *French Cuisine for All.* English Translation. Garden City, NY: Doubleday & Company, Inc., 1980.

Circletime Kids, "Pot au Feu"
  http://www.circletimekids.com/WorldLibrary/countries/France/recipes/FRA_Quiche.php

Circletime Kids, "Quiche"
  http://www.circletimekids.com/WorldLibrary/countries/France/recipes/FRA_Quiche.php

Europa, Panorama of the European Union.
  http://europa.eu/abc/panorama/index_en.htm

Fagan, Garrett C. "Claudius." Pennsylvania State University. April 2004.
  http://www.roman-emperors.org/claudius.htm

French History Timeline (Originally prepared for: http://www.uncg.edu/rom/courses/dafein/507/syllabus.htm)
  http://www.uncg.edu/rom/courses/dafein/civ/timeline.htm

Kreis, Steven. "Satan Triumphant: The Black Death." *The History Guide.* August 3, 2009.
  http://www.historyguide.org/ancient/lecture29b.html

Lascaux Cave
  http://www.lascaux.culture.fr/index.php?acc=true

Further Reading

Lavender Farm. The History of Lavender. Sources: Lavender by Elen Spector Platt, and Lavender: Practical Inspirations by Tess Evelegh, 2000.
http://www.lavenderfarm.com/history.htm

Le Cordon Bleu, Paris "A Brief History."
http://www.ibiblio.org/expo/restaurant/history.html

Levinson, Suzanne. "Pommes Frites." Food Network.com.
http://www.foodnetwork.com/recipes/follow-that-food/pommes-frites-recipe/index.html

Martin, Roger. *Discover Le Puy-en-Velay.* Vic-en-Bigorre, France: MSM, 1992

Middle Ages Religion
http://www.middle-ages.org.uk/middle-ages-religion.htm

One Way to Make a Paper Hat
http://www.herzogbr.net/fun/hat.htm

Steele, Ross. *When in France, Do as the French Do.* Columbus, OH: McGraw-Hill, 2002.

United Nations World Tourism Organization, UNWTO World Tourism Barometer, Interim Update, September 2009. UNWTO, Madrid, Spain
http://www.unwto.org/facts/eng/pdf/barometer/UNWTO_Barom09_update_sept_en.pdf

Universiteit Leiden. History of International Migration.
http://www.let.leidenuniv.nl/history/migration/chapter111.html

Van der Kamp, Gerald, Simone Hoog, and Daniel Meyer. Versailles: The *Château, the Gardens and Trianon.* Translated by Bronia Fuchs. New York: Vilo Inc., 1981.

On the Internet

A collection of links to many French-related websites
http://www.uni.edu/becker/french31.html

Fact Monster: France
http://www.factmonster.com/ipka/A0107517.html

Students of the World
http://www.studentsoftheworld.info/

PHOTO CREDITS: Cover, pp. 1, 4, 5, 7, 16, 19, 22, 32–34, 40, 41, 53, 54, 59—Creative Commons 2.0; pp. 2–3, 4—Photos.com; p. 11—Ch. THIOC, Gallo-Roman Museum, France; pp. 6, 10–12, 14, 15, 17, 18, 20–25, 27–29, 31, 35, 37–39, 44–47, 49, 51, 56–57—Amelia LaRoche; pp. 43, 52, 59—GettyImages. Every effort has been made to locate all copyright holders of material used in this book. If any errors or omissions have occurred, corrections will be made in future editions of the book.

accomplishment (uh-KOM-plish-munt)—Something that has been done successfully.

aristocratic (uh-ris-toh-KRAH-tik)—Grand and stylish; a high class in certain societies, including people who hold titles (such as "count" or "duchess").

controversial (kon-truh-VER-shul)—Prompting public disagreement.

Dark Ages (also called Early Middle Ages)—A period in Europe from about 500 to 1000 CE during which there was little artistic, scientific, or literary advancement.

devastated (DEH-vuh-stay-ted)—Destroyed or ruined.

dynasty (DY-nuh-stee)—A line of rulers who are related to each other.

enlightenment (en-LY-ten-munt)—The state of finding insight or new knowledge.

gastronomist (gas-TRAH-nuh-mist)—A gourmet, or food expert.

heretic (HAYR-ih-tik)—A person whose religious beliefs are in conflict with the teachings of the Roman Catholic Church.

High Middle Ages—The eleventh, twelfth, and thirteenth centuries in Europe.

illiterate (ih-LIH-tuh-rut)—Unable to read or write.

ingredient (in-GREE-dee-unt)—One part of something larger.

Late Middle Ages—The fourteenth and fifteenth centuries in Europe.

oppressive (oh-PREH-siv)—Weighing heavily on the mind or spirit; unfairly causing hardship.

opulent (AH-pyoo-lunt)—Wealthy, rich, and luxurious.

Paleolithic (pay-lee-oh-LIH-thik)—Relating to the earliest phase of the Stone Age, when humans began making ancient tools some three million years ago to the end of the Ice Age, around 8300 BCE.

prosperity (prah-SPAYR-ih-tee)—A state of abundance, or plenty for everyone.

reincarnation (ree-in-kar-NAY-shun)—The belief that the soul comes back to earth, again and again, in a different body each time.

renaissance (REH-nuh-zahntz)—The revival of art and literature; a rebirth, or new beginning.

Index

ABOUT THE
AUTHOR

Amelia LaRoche has traveled to France many times, most recently to visit family members there, including her wonderful nephew and niece. On one trip home after Christmas, customs officials refused to believe she had nothing to declare from this shopper's paradise, and they searched her luggage from top to bottom. She lives in New England with her three parrots and a newly acquired *cabot* from the animal shelter. *Cabot,* pronounced kah-BOH, is French for "mutt." More refined people use the word *chien* (shee-EH), which means "dog."